DEVOTIONS, PRAYERS & LIVING WISDOM

Saint
John
OF THE CROSS

Edited by Mirabai Starr

Sounds True, Inc., Boulder, CO 80306

© 2008 Mirabai Starr

Book designed by Lisa Kerans

Published 2008
Printed in Canada
ISBN 978-1-59179-796-8

Library of Congress Cataloging-in-Publication Data
Starr, Mirabai.
    Saint John of the Cross : devotions, prayers, and living
    wisdom / Mirabai Starr.
        p. cm.—(Devotions, prayers, and living wisdom series ;
    bk. six)
Includes bibliographical references.
ISBN 978-1-59179-796-8 (hardcover)
1. John of the Cross, Saint, 1542-1591—Prayers
    and devotions.
2. John of the Cross, Saint, 1542-1591. I. Title.

BX2167.J64S83 2008
248.2'2092—dc22
                                        2007042896

For a free catalog of wisdom teachings for the inner life,
call (800) 333-9185 or visit www.soundstrue.com.

*Dedicated to the
loving memory
of Ruth Ross*

Contents

Publisher's Note

Sounds True's *Devotions, Prayers, and Living Wisdom* series began with a desire to offer the essential teachings of great saints, mystics, and spiritual figures in a format that is compatible with meditation and contemplation. Each book contains poems, prayers, songs, and prose written by or in veneration of a figure who has transcended human confusion, and whose wisdom might awaken our own. It is our hope that these books will offer you insight, renewal, and companionship on the spiritual path.

Editor's Note

ark Night of the Soul, by the sixteenth-century Spanish mystic John of the Cross, has been the single most important spiritual book in my life. It embodies the perennial wisdom found at the heart of all the world's spiritual traditions: surrender into the absolute loving mystery of the Divine.

When I was a teenager, I became deeply involved in Sufism, the mystical branch of Islam. I was especially drawn to the Persian poet Rumi, who exquisitely harnessed the language of human love to express the yearning of the soul for union with God. In my early twenties, I encountered the Christian saint John of the Cross. I instantly recognized him as "the Rumi of Spain." John's ecstatic love poems to the Holy One echoed the transforming passion of his Sufi counterpart. Reading his poems in their original Spanish has been among the most powerful spiritual experiences of my life.

In 2002, I was given the privilege of translating *Dark Night of the Soul* into accessible English, which I followed with translations of John's spiritual mentor, Teresa of Avila. My focus as a translator of the Spanish mystics has been primarily on the prose teachings. It was not until I was asked to compile this book for Sounds True that I was given the opportunity to render a wider range of John's poetry.

John of the Cross claims—as all mystics do—that union with the Divine transcends all language and all concepts. Yet he devotes himself to the paradox of expressing the ineffable through the vehicle of mystical poetry. The results are so successful that his poems throw open the doors of the heart and invite the reader into a direct relationship with the Beloved. This poetry serves not only as a spiritual reminder, but also as a tangible tool for transformation.

In this book, I intersperse descriptive prose teachings with evocative poems. Many, though not all, of the translations are my own. Four themes rise to the surface of this mystical elixir: the longing of the soul for union with the Divine; the contemplative power of silence; the knowing that comes only from unknowing; and the wild, sweet dance of mystical love.

It is my prayer that the purity of these wisdom teachings strips all impediments from your mind, inviting you to meet your Beloved naked and free.

I am deeply grateful for the generous contributions and wise guidance of Father David Denny, Tessa Bielecki, Father Iain Matthew, Father Thomas Keating, Tim Farrington, Sara Morgan, Siddiq Hans von Briesen, Azima Melita Kolin, Kaysi Contreras, Sarah Jane Freymann, Kelly Notaras, and Haven Iverson.

— Mirabai Starr
August 2007

Opening Prayer

Praise to you,
Saint John of the Cross,
whose loving embrace of the mystery
teaches me to find sweet refuge
in the unknown
and the unknowable.
You quietly labored
to drain the cup of self
so that the Beloved could fill you.

Gentle monk,
with flames leaping in your heart,
light my way
through the dark night of my soul.
Let doubt become my ally,
and longing my friend.
Burn whatever stands between me
and union with the Beloved.

Thank you.

Amen.

— Mirabai Starr

ST·JOHN of the CROSS

Introduction

Juan de la Cruz was twenty-nine years old and madly in love with God.

The great living saint Teresa of Avila had recognized a rare sanctity and brilliance in this humble young friar and placed him in charge of her first reform convent.

Then, late one night, threatened by this movement to return the order to the contemplative path embodied by the Desert Fathers and Mothers, the mainstream Carmelites whisked him away and imprisoned him in Toledo.

His cell was a tiny closet that had formerly served as a latrine. There was not enough room to lie down, and the only window was far above his head. Through it, he could chart the course of three or four stars at a time as they passed slowly through space. Mostly, he sat very still in the darkness, shivering through the cold months, sweltering in the heat.

Twice a day, the friars took him out and flogged him.

"Denounce Teresa!" they demanded. "Renounce the heresy of this so-called reform!"

But he would not betray the dream. The dream of a life of voluntary simplicity, solitude, and silence. A contemplative life based on the Gospel teachings of poverty of spirit and charity of heart. A life of stripping away, rather than accumulating. Of relinquishing power and seeking nothing. Of nothing but loving friendship with the Divine and loving service to his creation.

When he was back in his cell, they would say terrible things in a stage whisper outside his door.

"Did you hear?" one friar would hiss to another. "Teresa of Avila has been arrested and her followers have all abandoned her. The reform has collapsed."

They were lying.

Other times they would mock the prisoner: "I guess your friends don't care about you after all, Father. Not a word from anyone. It appears you have been entirely forgotten, as if you never existed at all."

More lies.

He was not concerned about being remembered by human beings. But as the months ground by, he began to fear that he had been abandoned by the Holy One. For the first time in his life, he questioned the existence of a God he could no longer feel or remember And, as his soul dried up, he found he could no longer even conceive of this God to whom he had dedicated everything. Whenever he tried to pray, all he encountered was a cavernous emptiness.

He cried out, "Where have you hidden, my Beloved?"

Echoing from this cry came an outpouring of love poetry to God. He committed each poem to memory and recited them all again and again until they were etched on his heart. His poems became simultaneously

a call to and a response from his Beloved.
Little by little, into the darkness of
his isolation, the love of God flowed,
illuminating his shattered heart and filling
him with quiet joy.

At last, one dark night, a sympathetic
guard turned the other way as the frail friar
made his escape. Taking refuge among the
sisters in a nearby convent, he fell into an
ecstatic state, from which he never recovered.

༄ A Friar and a Half ༄

arly in the sixteenth century,
Gonzalo, a fair-skinned Spanish
nobleman from a family of textile
merchants, fell in love with Catalina, a North
African weaver-woman, who had come to
his door peddling cloth.

The Inquisition was at its pathological
height. Purity of European blood was
considered a sign of true devotion to the
Church. Jews and Muslims, who had been
living in Spain in relative harmony with

Christians under Islamic rule for many centuries, were being forced by the Roman Catholic Church to convert or be expelled from their homeland. Those *conversos* caught in the act of practicing their ancestral faith were often executed.

For a wealthy Spaniard to marry a Moor was an act of great courage, and Gonzalo's family disowned him as a result. This particular liaison was all the more risky in light of Gonzalo's own heritage: he probably came from a Jewish family, one that had successfully hidden its dangerous roots.

Juan de Yepes who would one day be known as St. John of the Cross, was the child of this great love. Born in 1542 in the small village of Fonteveros, near the city of Avila, John spent his early childhood wandering with his parents and his two older brothers in search of work. John's father, who apprenticed with his mother to learn the art of weaving, died of the plague when John was still a small boy. John's middle brother died of malnutrition soon after. Finally, his destitute mother settled what remained of her family in the teeming market town of Medina del Campo.

When John was twelve, he found work at a local hospital, caring for patients with incurable diseases, including many with syphilis. John found deep purpose and even solace in tending the dying. He bathed their sores, listened to their stories, and sang them the Arabic ballads he had learned as a child. He collected food and funds for the hospital and dedicated his life to embracing the people whom society had abandoned.

Don Alonso, the hospital administrator, was impressed by the young man's intelligence and sensitivity. In hopes that John might become a priest and harness his gifts in service to humanity, Don Alonso paid for his education at a Jesuit college and later at the legendary university of Salamanca. After completing his studies at age twenty-one, John joined a community of Carmelite friars, where he took the name John of the Cross. He was inspired by the example of the early thirteenth-century Carmelites of the Holy Land, an order whose rule of life flowed from a vision of contemplative prayer and voluntary simplicity. He was ordained as a priest in 1567.

But the sixteenth-century version of the Carmelite order had drifted far from its desert origins. Like other branches of the Roman Catholic Church, the Carmelites no longer placed primary emphasis on silence, stillness, and poverty. Convents were endowed by the dowries of wealthy nuns who couldn't find husbands, while the monks competed for who could perform the most spectacular penances. Quickly disenchanted by these realities, John was poised to leave the order and flee to the mountains to live as a hermit when a singular event changed the course of his life.

He met Teresa of Avila.

Teresa, the mother abbess of a Carmelite monastery, was twice John's age. Like John, Teresa longed for a return to the contemplative way of life lived by their forebears at the foot of Mount Carmel. Teresa was actively engaged in reforming the order when she heard of this fiery friar who shared her yearning for a community based on the cultivation of silent prayer and a direct relationship with the Divine.

Malnourished by childhood poverty, John's growth had been stunted and, as a twenty-five-year-old man, he stood barely five feet tall. After her first thrilling encounter with him, Teresa declared that, while he might be small in stature, John of the Cross was great in God. She referred to him as a "friar and a half" and considered him to be the father of her soul. John was the only man who ever fully understood Teresa, and she rested deeply in his understanding. John of the Cross joined Teresa of Avila's cause, and she immediately made him confessor to the nuns of her first convent.

John paid a high price for his devotion to Teresa and her reform movement. At twenty-nine, he was captured by a group of mitigated Carmelite friars. After nine months of incarceration and torture, he made a miraculous escape, tying shreds of knotted cloth into a rope and lowering himself through the tiny window of his cell and down the monastery wall. Uncertain where to go, he followed a dog who led him to a nearby convent of Teresa's nuns, who joyfully gave him sanctuary.

John of the Cross spent the next two decades in dedicated service to the vision he shared with Teresa, returning the attention of the monks and nuns he guided to the radiant stillness of their own souls. He was happiest when he was most invisible, praying alone in the chapel of nature, or addressing the spiritual yearnings of the nuns who adored him with humble lucidity.

Twenty years after his prison ordeal, John died of a recurring infection from the wounds he had sustained there. But during the period in between, he lived in ecstatic relationship to the Beloved. Love poetry flowed abundantly from his pen, and he radiated the bliss of perpetual union with the Divine, touching everyone in his sphere with his deep stillness and playful wisdom.

*Even though this holy night darkens the
spirit, it does so only to light up everything.*

— St. John of the Cross,
Dark Night of the Soul

ometimes in the spiritual life, if you
are very lucky, the Holy One slams
the door shut and plunges you
into darkness.

This may occur when you are at your
best, basking in the glow of tender feelings
of devotion in prayer and practice, when,
all at once, the ancient teachings of the
masters make perfect sense. You find your
old ego has become less cantankerous and
is giving you more moments of peace.
You are beginning to entertain notions of
being a guide to others. People seem to be
drawn toward your natural equanimity and
inspiring way with words.

But, suddenly, God bores you. Suddenly,
you do not have any idea who this God even *is*.

Spiritual practice turns out to be more tedious than a teeth-cleaning, and just about as holy. Studying sacred literature feels like reading an economics textbook from the 1950s. Where not long ago you sat in the cathedral singing to God, tears of joy streaming down your face, now your heart has turned to stone and you have stopped going to church. You used to be able to meditate for an hour and it felt like five minutes. Now you watch the clock as the minutes limp by and finally decide to get up off the cushion and go back to bed.

What's happening here? You suspect you have been very bad and God is punishing you, if he even exists at all, which is beginning to seem more and more unlikely. You resign yourself to abandonment. If you were God, you would give up on you, too, worthless wretch that you are.

You decide to confide in a couple of spiritual people you know. They smile knowingly and assure you that everyone grapples with periods of dryness and obscurity along the spiritual journey. They affirm your basic goodness and remind you that you are not so special that God would forsake you and nobody else. They quote from the *Cloud of Unknowing* and the *Heart Sutra*. Their words only make you feel worse. It's obvious that they have never felt what you are feeling and do not understand you at all.

You withdraw into yourself.

Which is exactly where God wants you.

❧

Even though [this dark night] humbles her and makes her miserable, it is only to raise her up and exalt her.

— St. John of the Cross,
Dark Night of the Soul

❧

You stop fighting and, exhausted, rest in the darkness of unknowing. You have been drained and shattered. You sit in your brokenness and listen to the sound of your own breathing. There is nothing else to do. There is nowhere else to be.

Into this darkness of the soul, you begin to notice a subtle inflowing of sweetness and ease. The ancient mystics call this surrender "infused contemplation." Finally empty, you are free to receive the Holy One. This new peace is not the fruit of an active practice of meditation. It is a fully receptive state. Your only job is simply to be. The Holy One will do all the rest.

He has purified you with his fire—stripped away all attachments to how spiritual experience is supposed to feel and obliterated all mental constructs about what God is supposed to mean. He transmits his secret teachings of love, making you ready for union with him. Infused with his grace, you realize that what your old eyes mistook for darkness, your new eyes recognize as pure light.

*Even though it impoverishes her, emptying
her of natural inclinations, it is only so
she will reach out for the divine and freely
enjoy the fruits of all things, of above and
of below.*

— St. John of the Cross,
Dark Night of the Soul

B. JOANNES À CRUCE.

Chapter One

Longing

*I*t begins with the wrenching feeling
that you—quite understandably—
mistake for separation from your
divine source.

Which it isn't.

*It's Abraham and Sarah throwing a
feast in honor of the weaning of their
baby boy. It's Abraham and Sarah
celebrating and giving thanks for their
healthy child, Isaac, while he lies wailing in
his little chair, refusing to eat his crusty
bread and lentils.*

*It feels as if the most beautiful lover in
the world had come into your life, wooed
you with perfect poetry and electric kisses,
promised you were the one, the one and only,
and then disappeared in the middle of the
night without a word.*

But this is a lover who will never leave you.

The lover has only gone to prepare your wedding chamber. Soon your betrothal will be consummated—and in the sweetest way you could possibly imagine. No, far sweeter than that. Your ecstasy will catapult you beyond yourself. You are a mountain stream rushing toward the sea, which is your lover, rising joyfully to meet you.

But for now, you do not know this. You cannot know this. You know only unbearable yearning. You have forgotten that the longing itself is the answer to the longing. That in the very crying out for the Holy One, the Holy One is pouring himself into you.

Where have you hidden away,
Beloved, and left me grieving, care on care?
Hurt me and wouldn't stay
but off like a deer from there?
I hurried forth imploring the empty air.

You shepherds, you that rove
over the range where mountains touch the sky,
if you should meet my love
—my one love—tell him why
I'm faint, in a fever, and may die.

— St. John of the Cross,
in "The Spiritual Canticle"

⚭ Words That Comfort God ⚭

I won't go to sleep tonight until you have spoken to me
those words that you read to yourself
when you need
comfort,
God.

This ceiling post in my room, I will tie my hands to it.
If I sleep it will be standing passed out
in exhaustion from vigil
and prayer.

I don't know, you tell me, Beloved,
how to win your
body,

for I have tried everything, but I
feel so helpless.

I will not lie in my bed again until you have kissed me
with those words that you whisper to yourself,
my Lord, when you need comfort,

when you need
comfort.

—In the spirit of St. John of the Cross,
Daniel Ladinsky

༄ God the Mother ༄

Surrendering to God, says John, is
like letting down into the arms of
an unconditionally loving mother.
God the Mother holds the baby soul close,
warming it with the heat of her breasts,
and strokes its tender face. She nourishes
the soul with sweet milk and softened foods.

As the soul grows, God the Mother
gradually begins to hide her tender love.
She caresses the baby less. She removes the
soul's mouth from her breast and sets the
child down on its own shaky legs. This helps
the young soul let go of childish ways and
face things as they are.

Beginners on the path home to the
Holy One are like infants. The Loving God
pours grace into the newly surrendered
soul. In this loving flow, the soul tastes
the sweetness of the God and effortlessly
drinks in the divine essence. Grace kindles
the soul's ardor for serving God. Grace
gives the soul intense delight in spiritual

*practice. When the soul participates in
these blessed activities, God the Mother
places her breast tenderly into the mouth
of her child and nurtures it. The baby
grows strong and vigorous.*

*Yet, when the time for weaning comes—
as it must, as it should—the young soul
does not feel ready to let go. It experiences
this natural shift as abandonment.*

⤜⤜⤜ Is That My Fate? ⤜⤜⤜

. . . The flame called the moth but the glass pane was there.
How many have died not in the fire but in the cold,
crazed in longing.

—In the spirit of St. John of the Cross,
Daniel Ladinsky

Keep north, you winds of death.
Come, southern wind, for lovers. Come and stir
the garden with your breath.
Shake the fragrance on the air.
My love will feed among the lilies there.

— St. John of the Cross,
in "The Spiritual Canticle"

[In prison] John was a child.

He had been hauled beyond the threshold
of his own resources, taken to those outer
limits where the only alternatives are a Spirit
who fills, or chaos.

It was as if the anesthetic which normal life
provides had worn off, his inner self had been
scraped bare, and now he ached in a way he
never had before for a God who was utterly
beyond him.

This was the real wound, and it drew from
him a raw cry, "Where are you?"

— Father Iain Matthew,
in *The Impact of God*

⁓ No Hope ⁓

*T*he soul that is plunged into the
stormy night, where so many
blessings are born, is fortunate,
says John, but she still deserves
compassion. She thinks she is drowning.

The soul in the dark night is engulfed by
feelings of utter desolation and unmitigated
solitude. Even if she is lucky enough to
have a spiritual guide who understands
something of this blessed state, she is, by
definition, inconsolable.

There is neither a teacher alive nor a
theological doctrine ever revealed that can
offer a shred of support or solace.

"Take comfort," says her spiritual
director. "These sufferings of yours signify
great blessings."

But a thousand enlightened beings
could all line up and offer a thousand good
reasons why this terrifying emptiness is
evidence of grace and she would not believe
them. She cannot.

Sinking ever deeper into anguish, the soul in the dark night is convinced that her guides are saying these hopeful things because they are not seeing and feeling what she is seeing and feeling, so they cannot possibly understand her. Their efforts to relieve her pain only intensify it.

The truth is, says John, that there is no way out. Until the Holy One finishes his work of stripping the soul of everything that stands between her and himself, there is no remedy, there is no relief. If a single glimmer of hope remained, the purification would not be authentic.

ᴄᴍᴍᴏ Ϻy Soul Is a Candle ᴄᴍᴍᴏ

My soul is a candle that burned away the veil;
only the glorious duties of light I now have.

The sufferings I knew initiated me into God.
I am a holy confessor for men.

When I see their tears running across their cheeks
and falling into
His hands,

what can I say to their great sorrow
that I too have
known.

The soul is a candle that will burn away the darkness,
only the glorious duties of love we
will have.

The sufferings I knew initiated me into God.
Only His glorious cares
I now have.

—In the spirit of St. John of the Cross,
Daniel Ladinsky

O Lord, my God,
who will seek you
with simple and pure love
and not find you are all
    he desires,
for you show yourself first
and go out to meet those
who desire you . . .

       — St. John of the Cross,
       in *Sayings of Love and Light*

Newness of Being

God heals the soul, John tells us, by killing her. The Holy One dips his hand into the bitter solvent of purification and lifts it over the soul, letting it rain down on her, cleansing and healing her, making her die to all that is not inherently divine.

When the soul is stripped bare of her old skin, John promises, the Holy One clothes her afresh. She is draped in newness of being. God revitalizes her youth and sets her free, just as he fashions the tail feathers for the eagle and releases her into the sky, empowering her to soar.

The moment of purgation is a moment of agony, but only because we cling to our old skin, afraid that without it we will cease to exist.

And we are correct.

Who we thought we were must perish, so that who we really are may rise up, radiant and pure. Who we really are is identical with that which we come from: divine love. Boundless.

Mary Magdalene, in spite of her past, paid
no attention to the men at the banquet.
It made no difference to her if they were
prominent or common. She did not consider
whether it was proper for her to go sobbing
and shedding tears among the guests.

Her only concern was to reach the
one who had wounded her soul and set it
on fire. No, she could not wait for a more
opportune time!

The intoxication of love gives the soul
crazy courage.

Knowing that her Beloved was sealed in
a tomb by an enormous rock, surrounded
by guards posted just in case the disciples
would try to steal his body, Mary did not let
anything stand in the way of her going out
at daybreak to anoint him with ointments.

Finally, the inebriating power of her love-
longing compelled Mary to ask a man she
thought was a gardener if he had stolen him
and, if he had, where he had put him so that

she could take him back. She did not pause to consider that, by the light of sound judgment, her question sounded ridiculous . . .

— St. John of the Cross,
in *Dark Night of the Soul*

Oh who my grief can mend!
Come and make the last surrender that I
    yearn for,
And let there be an end
Of messengers you send
Who bring me other tidings than I
    burn for.

All those that haunt the spot
Recount your charm, and wound me
    worst of all
Babbling I know not what
Strange rapture, they recall,
Which leaves me stretched and dying
    where I fall.

— St. John of the Cross,
in "The Spiritual Canticle"

A solitary shepherd
withdrew in his grief.
His thoughts drifted far
from any memory of joy
and came to rest on his shepherdess.
Love had shattered his heart.

It was not the wound that made him cry out,
nor the fact that the arrow had been launched—
although it lodged deep in the most tender
heart of his heart.
He wept because his beloved
had forgotten him.

The mere thought
that he had become invisible
to the one he loved
had driven him to foreign lands,
where he fought in a war
he did not believe in,
begging for a physical wound
to obliterate the anguish in his heart.

"Woe be to the stranger
who has stolen my darling,"
he said to no one.
"She will not even look in my eyes.
She does not acknowledge
the love that shatters my heart."

A long time passed.
Suddenly the shepherd leapt to his feet
and climbed a tree.
He stretched his beautiful arms open wide
and courageously suspended himself in
    its branches,
until death liberated him at last
from the love that shattered his heart.

— St. John of the Cross

The dark night descends on a soul only when everything else has failed.

This, says John, is the beginning of blessedness. This is the choiceless choice when the soul can do nothing but surrender.

Because, even if you cannot sense a shred of the Beloved's love for you, even if you can scarcely conjure up your old passion for him, it has become perfectly clear that you are incapable of doing anything on your own to remedy your spiritual brokenness.

All efforts to purge your unspiritual inclinations have only honed the laser of attention on the false self.

Unwilling to keep struggling, the soul finds itself surrendering to its deepest inner wound and breathing in the stillness there.

— Mirabai Starr,
in the Introduction to *Dark Night of the Soul*

⚕ Darkening the Light ⚕

*J*ust when the soul is starting to really enjoy the spiritual journey and the divine sun is lighting every step of her path, John says, the Holy One suddenly plunges her into darkness. He slams the door shut. He cuts her off from the source of sweet spiritual waters she has been drinking as often and as deeply as she desired.

How could he? she fumes. Haven't I been cultivating virtues and resisting base temptations? Haven't I persevered in prayer and meditation when I would have rather been sleeping an extra hour or watching television? The more I have practiced spiritual discipline, the more pleasure I have derived from these practices and the more swiftly my worldly cravings have fallen away. What have I done wrong?

Nothing, the Holy One whispers. You have done nothing wrong, my love.

*Rather, I see that you have grown a
little. You no longer need to suckle from
the divine breast. Here. I will take off these
baby clothes that swaddle you and set you
free. Walk. Walk to me, my beloved one.*

*But the soul feels like she's walking
backwards, and she wails in protest.*

Tracking your sandal-mark
The maidens search the roadway for your sign,
Yearning to catch the spark
And taste the scented wine
Which emanates a balm that is divine.

Deep-cellared is the cavern
Of my love's heart, I drank of him alive:
Now stumbling from the tavern,
No thoughts of mine survive,
And I have lost the flock I used to drive.

— St. John of the Cross,
in "The Spiritual Canticle"

Let My Eyes
See Your Face

How manage breath on breath
so long, my soul, not living where life is?
Brought low and close to death
by those arrows of his?
Love was the bow. I know. I have witnesses.

And wounds to show. You'd cleave
clean to the heart, and never think of healing?
Steal it, and when you leave
leave it? What sort of dealing,
to steal and never keep, and yet keep stealing?

O shorten the long days
of burning thirst—no other love allays them.
Let my eyes see your face,
treasure to daze them.
Except for love, it's labor lost to raise them.

> — St. John of the Cross,
> in " The Spiritual Canticle"

ᗧᗢᑐ Rare Bird ᗧᗢᑐ

The olive hermit thrush,
Unseen in summer alamos
Above the cold creek rush;
At his song the woods fall hush;
All ache and fire, he pines for his esposa.

— Father David M. Denny,
in honor of St. John of the Cross

alamos: cottonwood trees
esposa: spouse

The Beloved has always revealed
the treasures of his wisdom
and his spirit
to humanity.

But now that the face of malevolence
bares itself
more and more,
so does the Beloved
bare his treasures
more and more.

— St. John of the Cross,
in *Sayings of Love & Light*

ꙮꙮꙮ Ray of Darkness ꙮꙮꙮ

Why, John asks, is the action of divine light, which purges the soul of delusion and illumines her, called the "dark night"?

Divine wisdom is a ray of darkness that pierces the veil of ignorance. This light so utterly transcends the soul's natural faculties that it appears to the soul as darkness. It conquers her intellect and stills it.

When the soul has not become fully empty of her small self, the ray of darkness feels like a shroud dropping over her eyes. Her ordinary mind is impoverished and bereft. Her divine mind has not yet awakened. She is terrified.

When the soul has been transformed, the illuminating ray of secret wisdom lights up her entire being and quietly radiates throughout the heavens and the earth. The cover of darkness lifts, allowing the soul to see with perfect clarity.

O soul,
most beautiful among all creatures,
you who so long to know the place
where your Beloved is,
so as to seek him
and become one with him,
now it has been stated:

you yourself are the home in
    which he dwells.

Here is a reason to be happy;
here is a cause for joy:
the realization that every blessing
and all you hope for
is so close to you
as to be within you.

Be glad,
find joy there,
gathered together
and present to him
who dwells within,
since he is so close to you;

desire him there,
adore him there,
and do not go off
looking for him elsewhere . . .

There is just one thing:
even though he is within you,
he is hidden.

— St. John of the Cross,
in "The Spiritual Canticle"

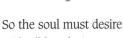

So the soul must desire
with all her desire
to come to what in this life lies
beyond her mind or the
capacity
of her heart.

— St. John of the Cross,
in *Ascent to Mount Carmel*

In the first place, you should realize that, if the person is seeking God, much more is her Beloved seeking her.

So the soul must understand that God's desire in all the good things he does to her . . . is to prepare her for further anointings . . . more like him in quality, until she comes to such purity, such refined readiness, that she merits union with God . . .

— St. John of the Cross,
in *Living Flame of Love*

The Essence of Desire

I did not
have to ask my heart what it wanted,
because of all the desires I have ever known just one did I cling to
for it was the essence of
all desire:

to hold beauty in
my soul's
arms.

—In the spirit of St. John of the Cross,
Daniel Ladinsky

And on to our eyrie then,
in grottos of the rock, high, high!
    Old rumor placed it
far beyond the wit of men.
Ah, but we've traced it,
and wine of the red pomegranate—
    there we'll taste it!

There finally you'll show
the very thing my soul was yearning for;
and the same moment, O
my dearest life, restore
something you gave the other day: once more

the breathing of the air,
the nightingale in her affectionate vein,
woods and the pleasure there
in night's unruffled reign—
these, and the flames embracing without pain.

— St. John of the Cross,
in "The Spiritual Canticle"

Longing

There he made gently free;
had honey of revelation to confide.
There I gave all of me;
hid nothing, had no pride;
there I promised to become his bride.

Forever at his door
I gave my heart and soul. My fortune too.
I have no flock anymore,
no other work in view.
My only occupation: love. It's all I do.

If I'm not seen again
in the old places, on the village ground,
say of me: lost to men.
Say I'm adventure-bound
for love's sake. Lost on purpose to be found.

— St. John of the Cross,
in "The Spiritual Canticle"

Chapter Two

Silence

༄ Be Nothing ༄

Be still, and remember that I AM. The reason the Sabbath is a commandment is because the Holy One knew we would never voluntarily lay down our burdens and simply BE.

Lay them down.

Carve out a day every week, or an hour a day, or a moment each hour, and abide in loving silence with the Friend. Feel the frenetic concerns of life in the world fall away, like the last leaves of autumn being lifted from the tree in the arms of a zephyr.

Be the bare tree.

Be nothing. Not in the sense that you are unworthy, but the opposite. The Holy One loves you so much that he has invited you into his secret chamber to be alone with you. He has stripped you of yourself

and taken you inside him. What a blessing!
What an honor! To be made nothing.

Let your breath become a tiny bird
playing very lightly at the tip of your
nose. Let your gaze turn inward. Stop
worrying about what's for dinner, which
bills have been paid, how your friend
has not returned your call (is she mad at
you?), whether your teenager is clinically
depressed or just temporarily ravaged by
passing hormones.

Feel your attention drifting gently back
to your hidden core, your empty cave, your
naked bones, your true home. Give thanks.

What we need most
in order to make progress
is to be silent
before this great God
with our appetites
and our tongue.

For the language
he best hears
is silent love.

— St. John of the Cross,
in *Maxims on Love*

The dove so snowy-white,
Returning to the Ark, her frond bestows:
And seeking to unite
The mate of her delight
Has found him where the shady river flows.

In solitude she bided,
And in the solitude her nest she made:
In solitude he guided
His loved one through the shade
Whose solitude the wound of love
    has made.

— St. John of the Cross,
in "The Spiritual Canticle"

Bridle your tongue
and your thoughts
very much.

Direct your affection
habitually
toward God.

Then
your spirit
will be
divinely enkindled.

— St. John of the Cross,
in *Maxims on Love*

Those whom God begins to lead into the
solitude of the [inner] desert are like the
Children of Israel. God gave them manna
from heaven to eat, which contained within
itself all flavors and turned into the taste
each of them most hungered for.

Still, all they could feel was their craving
for the meats and onions they ate in Egypt.
This is what they were used to, and this
is what they preferred over the delicate
sweetness of the angelic manna. In the
midst of that divine food, they wept and
sighed for flesh . . .

Our appetite can be so base that it makes
us long for our own wretched rations, repulsed
by incomparable heavenly plenitude . . .

If only souls that this happens to could
just be quiet, setting aside all concern
about accomplishing any task—interior
or exterior—and quit troubling themselves
about doing anything!

Soon, within that very stillness and
release, they would begin to taste subtly of
that interior nourishment, a nourishment so
delicate that if they were purposely to try,
they could never taste it.

— St. John of the Cross,
in *Dark Night of the Soul*

[God] spoke one word . . . and this word he is always speaking in eternal silence. It is in silence that the soul must hear it.

— St. John of the Cross

Without support and with support,
without light and living
    in darkness,
I am utterly being consumed.

My soul is loosed
from all created things,
and raised above itself,
and in a delectable life
brought near to God alone . . .

and although I suffer in shadows
in this mortal life,
my misfortune is not so great,
because, though I lack the light,
I have eternal life;

for the devoted soul possesses
the love of such a life,
when he becomes more blind,
without light and living
  in darkness.

Love did such work in me
after I knew her,
that, if there be good or bad in me,
all is made into one savor,
and the soul transformed in her;

and thus, in her delicious flame,
which I feel within my soul,
swiftly, without sparing a thing,
I am utterly being consumed.

— St. John of the Cross

Say when you were very young the veil
lifted just enough for you to glimpse the
underlying Real behind it and then
dropped again.

Maybe it never recurred, but you could
not forget.

And this discovery became the prime mover of the rest of your life, in ways you may not have even noticed . . .

Say prayer starts to dry up on your tongue. Sacred literature becomes fallen leaves, blows away. Meditation brings no serenity anymore. Devotion grows brittle, cracks. The God you bow down to no longer draws you.

Say you bow down anyway . . .

Say each of the familiar rooms you go to seeking refuge are dark now, and empty. You sit down anyway.

You take off your clothes at the door and enter naked. All agendas have fallen away. You grow so still in your non-doing that you forget for a moment that you *are* or that maybe God is *not*.

This quietude deepens in proportion to your surrender . . .

It is only in this vast emptiness that he can enter, as your Beloved, and fill you. Where the darkness is nothing but unutterable radiance . . .

— Mirabai Starr,
in the Introduction to *Dark Night of the Soul*

Jesus be in your soul, my [friend] in Christ.

Thanks indeed for your letter; and thanks be to God for wanting to make use of you in [our community]. It is His Majesty who has done this, to bring you to greater profit.

For the more he wants to give, the more he makes us desire, till he leaves us empty so as to fill us with blessings . . .

God's immense blessings can only fit into a heart that is empty. They come in that kind of solitude.

For this reason, the Lord would love to see you, since he loves you well, well and truly alone, intent on being himself all your company.

And [you] will have to take heart and be content only with his company, in order to find all contentment in that; for even if a person were in heaven, if she didn't align her will to want it, she wouldn't be content.

— St. John of the Cross

When the dark night descends, the soul loses her desire to do much of anything. She is not depressed, exactly. She is not really tired, either. Rather, a deep stillness has fallen over her, and she doesn't want to move a muscle or think a thought. Formless quietude feels much more compelling than formal prayer.

But she is plagued by the belief that she should be doing something.

If the soul tries to force her faculties to engage at a time like this, John teaches us, she will squander the gift of peace God is infusing in her. All she needs to do is rest in it.

John compares the soul in this state to an artist's model. Say a master painter was composing a portrait and the model kept changing positions because she thought she wasn't contributing anything by staying in one position. Rather than helping the master, she would be disturbing him, and preventing him from accomplishing his masterpiece.

Stop moving. Let God gaze on you.

To come to savor all,
seek to find savor in nothing;
to come to possess all,
seek possession in nothing;
to come to be all;
seek in all to be nothing . . .
to come to what you know not,
you must go by a way where you
know not . . .
to come to what you are not
you must go by a way where you are not.

— St. John of the Cross,
in *Ascent to Mount Carmel*

Just as Abraham made a great feast when
his son Isaac was weaned, so there is
rejoicing in heaven when God removes the
baby clothes from the soul.

He is setting her down from his arms
and making her walk on her own two feet.
He removes her lips from the milky breast

and replaces the soft, sweet mush of infants
with the crusty bread of the robust . . .

The time when the soul went about all
dressed up for a party was a time when she
found plenty of gratification and support
from God in spiritual practice. She was
happy and satisfied then, convinced that
she was, in some way, serving him.

Now, dressed in the working clothes of
aridity and desolation, all her earlier lights
darkened, the soul shines more clearly in
the virtue of self-knowledge . . .

Innumerable blessings flow from
the fountain that is the source of self-
knowledge to the soul that is humbly
clothed in the cloak of aridity.

— St. John of the Cross,
in *Dark Night of the Soul*

We please the Holy One more
with one act of goodness, however small,
that we commit in secret,
not even wishing
that someone would notice,
than with a thousand good deeds
done with the hope of recognition.

The person who works for the Holy One
with the purest love
is not only uninterested
in the approval of other human beings
but she does not even expect God to notice.

Even if she thought
that God would never know
what she had done for him,
such a person would not cease to offer him
every loving thing
with the same joy and purity of heart.

> — St. John of the Cross,
> in *Sayings of Love & Light*

They'll be thinking it was all rather
special, and that God had spoken; and it
will have been little more than nothing, or
nothing, or less than nothing.

Because if something does not give birth
to humility, and love, and dying to self, and
godly simplicity, and silence—what can it be?

— St. John of the Cross,
in *Ascent to Mount Carmel*

Lose yourself in remembrance
of the Creator
and let the creation go.
Turn your attention inward
and dwell in love with the Beloved.

— St. John of the Cross

ꙮ Stop Thinking ꙮ

When the dark night descends on the soul, its radiance blinds the intellect. She can no longer formulate concepts. She doesn't even want to. It is tempting to consider this inability to engage the intellect as a failing. It is easy to assume that you are wasting time.

Do not force it, says John. Stop thinking. Drop down into a state of formless quietude and abide there. This is no time, he says, for discursive meditation. No time for pondering theological doctrines or asserting articles of faith.

Your only task now is to set your soul free. Take a break from ideas and knowledge. Unencumbered by the burden of the analytical mind, you don't need to bother with thinking and meditating.

Content yourself with a loving attentiveness toward the Holy One. This requires no effort, no agitation, no desire to taste him or feel him or understand him.

Patiently persevere in this state of prayer that has no name.

"Trust in God," John says, "who does not abandon those who seek him with a simple and righteous heart."

By doing nothing now, the soul accomplishes great things.

༄ **Peace** ༄

Quiet yourself.
Reach out with your mind's skillful hand.
Let it go inside of me
and touch
God.

Don't
be shy, dear.
Every aspect of Light we are meant
to know.

The calm hand holds more
than baskets of goods
from the market.

The calm soul knows more
than anything this world
can offer from her
beautiful
womb.

—In the spirit of St. John of the Cross,
Daniel Ladinsky

The central paradox of the spiritual path
is that in striving to transcend the self,
we actually build it up. Our holy solutions
invariably calcify into grotesque casts
of ego.

The dark night is God's solution to
our solutions, dissolving our best-laid
constructions anew into the mystery
of grace.

It happens in spite of our best efforts
to resist it. But thank God it happens.

—Tim Farrington,
in *A Hell of Mercy*

Chapter Three

Unknowing

*I*t is time to enter the desert.
You may not take anything with
you: not your insulated bottle
of cool water, not a knife, not a single
raisin. You may not take a sleeping bag.
No cell phone or map. Leave the sunscreen
behind. Burn.

It is time to enter into utter unknowing.
And, by unknowing, you will come to
know truly.

The mind is an impediment on this
journey. The senses are misleading. Leave
them on the porch when you slip away in
the middle of the night. Be very quiet as you
close the door behind you. The members of
your household will not understand your
quest. They will try to keep you home.
Leave. Go now.

No one claims this will be an easy journey. Your senses will thirst for the familiar juices that remind them of a time when the Holy One fed them from his own breasts. The intellect will grope around in the dark, panicking. Pay no attention. Walk through the night. Sit very still in the daytime and watch the miracle of your breath as it quietly fills your lungs, and empties them again.

Spend forty days in the wilderness, and forty nights. Don't give up. The worst that will happen is that you will die.

Die to your fragmented self and be reborn into your divine self. Enter knowing through the needle of unknowing. In silence, finally hearing the voice of the Holy One. In surrendering to sheer emptiness, being filled with the Beloved at last.

Oh, what a difficult life this can be! We live in such danger and it is so hard to find the truth!

What is clear and true, we experience as opaque and doubtful. We flee from what we need the most. We embrace whatever fills us with satisfaction and run after the worst thing for us, falling down with every step.

What danger we live in! The light of our natural eyes is supposed to be our guide, but it is the first thing to mislead us on our journey to God.

What we have to do is to keep our eyes shut and walk the path in darkness if we want to be sure where we are going . . .

— St. John of the Cross,
in *Dark Night of the Soul*

The Sleeping
Man Is Blessed

. . . The sleeping man is blessed with
a faith that is not
active.

Faith as it ripens turns into an almost insatiable appetite,

and the awake lion must prowl for God
in places it once
feared.

—In the spirit of St. John of the Cross,
Daniel Ladinsky

I would not sacrifice my soul
for all the beauty of this world.

There is only one thing
for which I would risk everything:
an I-don't-know-what
that lies hidden
in the heart of the Mystery.

The taste of finite pleasure
leads nowhere.
All it does is exhaust the appetite
and ravage the palate.
And so I would not sacrifice
    my soul
for all the sweetness of this world.

But I would risk everything
for an I-don't-know-what
that lies hidden
in the heart of the Mystery.

The generous heart
does not collapse into the
        easy things,
but rises up in adversity.
It settles for nothing.
Faith lifts it higher and higher.

Such a heart savors
an I-don't-know-what
found only in the heart of
        the Mystery.

The soul that God has touched
burns with love-longing.
Her tastes have been transfigured.
Ordinary pleasures sicken her.
She is like a man with a fever:
nothing tastes good anymore.

All she wants
is an I-don't-know-what
locked in the heart of
        the Mystery . . .

I will never lose myself
for anything the senses can taste,
nor for anything the mind
    can grasp,
no matter how sublime,
    how delicious.
I will not pause for beauty,
I will not linger over grace.
I am bound for
an I-don't-know-what
deep within the heart of
    the Mystery.

— St. John of the Cross

Worthless
∽ Accomplishments ∽

*T*he lions at the gates become more ferocious the closer we get to home.

The fragmented self, says John, grows increasingly tricky as the soul approaches union with God. It begins to create little displays of spiritual power to seduce the soul into thinking she is accomplishing something of importance. It stirs her lust for rituals and ceremonies, not because these things strip away all that separates the soul from her Beloved, but in fact for the opposite reason: to build up her pride and presumption.

The soul begins to suffer from the illusion that she is special, which stops her in her tracks. The fragmented self wipes its brow in relief.

The fragmented self suffers from its own illusion—the illusion of separation from God. It fears the annihilation of divine union. And so, as the soul slowly awakens to its divine destiny, the fragmented self must do everything in its power to keep her from going home. Its tricks grow more subtle and insidious, taking the form of spiritual accomplishments.

It knows quite well that such powers are not only worthless, but they can easily become vices.

Upon a quest of love,
hope sturdy and steadfast,
I flew so high, so high,
I caught the prey at last.

In this divine affair,
to triumph—if I might—
I had to soar so high
I vanished out of sight.
Yet in the same ascent
my wings were failing fast—
but love arose so high
I caught the prey at last.

Just when this flight of mine
had reached its highest mark,
my eyes were dazzled so
I conquered in the dark.
I gave a blind black surge
for love—my self surpassed!
And went so high, so high
I caught the prey at last.

Saint John of the Cross

The higher up I went
there, in this dizzy game,
the lower I appeared,
more humble, weak, and lame.
I cried, But none can win!
and sinking fast oh fast
yet went so high, so high,
I caught the prey at last.

Then—marvelous!—I made
a thousand flights in one,
for hope of heaven will see
all it can wish, be done.
I hoped for this alone;
I hoped; was not downcast.
And went so high, so high,
I caught the prey at last.

— St. John of the Cross

❧

The fly
that clings to honey
hinders its flight.

The soul
that allows itself attachment
to spiritual sweetness
hinders its own liberty
and contemplation.

— St. John of the Cross,
in *Sayings of Love & Light*

Oh, spiritual soul! When you see that your desires are darkened, your inclinations dried up, and your faculties incapacitated, do not be disturbed. Consider it grace.

God is freeing you from yourself. He is taking the matter from your hands. No matter how well these hands have served you, they are still clumsy and unclean.

Never before could you labor as effectively as you can now when you put

down your burden and let God take your
hand and guide you through the darkness
as though you were blind, leading you to a
place you do not know.

Who cares how good your hands and
feet may be?

— St. John of the Cross,
in *Dark Night of the Soul*

If you want to find a hidden treasure you
must enter the hiding place secretly, and
once you have discovered it, you will also be
hidden as the treasure is hidden.

Since, then, your beloved Bridegroom
is a treasure hidden in a field for which the
wise merchant sold all his possessions [as
Jesus tells us in the Gospels] and that field
is your soul, in order to find him you should
forget all your possessions and all creatures
and hide in the secret inner room of your spirit.

— St. John of the Cross,
in "The Spiritual Canticle"

I discovered the science
of perfect peace, perfect holiness!
A direct path opened
through the heart of solitude.
Speechless,
I walked into the unknown.

This journey transcends all thought.

I was so intoxicated,
so totally absorbed,
so completely enraptured,
all my senses were drained of sensation
and my spirit was filled
with an understanding beyond
    understanding.

This awareness transcends all thought.

Whoever arrives
in the land of unknowing
frees herself of herself.
Everything she thought she knew
falls away

and her consciousness expands
to enfold the whole universe.

This circle transcends all thought.

The higher she ascends,
the less she understands.
The dark cloud
that lights up the night
reveals itself
as pure mystery.
The knower
rests
in unknowing.

This dark light transcends all thought.

Such knowing by unknowing
is so exalted, so potent,
that there is not a thinker alive
who can grasp it with his mind.
Who can reach that high?
We can only understand by
    not understanding.

This wisdom transcends all thought.

It is a science so exalted,
a study so sublime,
that no human faculty can contain it.
The only way to attain it
is to plunge into the unknown.

This leap transcends all thought.

Listen:
this sacred understanding
lies in a single sip
of the Divine Essence.
Knowing by unknowing
is an act of mercy
the Beloved pours on us.

This mercy transcends all thought.

— St. John of the Cross

Mystical wisdom hides the soul inside herself.

Sometimes it so thoroughly engulfs her in its secret abyss that the soul clearly sees herself as being carried far away from all she has ever known.

She feels she is being led to a vast wilderness which no human creature can reach—an immense, unbounded desert.

The deeper and more solitary it is, the more lovely and delicious.

— St. John of the Cross,
in *Dark Night of the Soul*

How intimately I know the spring
that rushes and flows
in the depths of the night.

Its everlasting source is hidden.

How well I know the way
to that secret land from which she rises
through the depths of the night.

I do not know her origin, for she has none.

Yet how deeply I know that she is the
    original origin,
the place from which all beginnings begin,
in the depths of the night.

There is nothing as beautiful as this.

The earth and the skies
drink from her waters
in the depths of the night.

Who can fathom her? She is bottomless.
Who can cross her? There is no bridge.
She mingles with the depths of the night.

Her clarity can never be obscured.
All light emanates from her,
even in the depths of the night.

I have known her voluminous currents.

Her streams rush
through the heavens and the hell realms.
All beings dip into her
in the depths of the night.

Great streams flow from great sources.

The current born from this first fountain
is all-powerful.
It surges in the depths of the night . . .

The waters are singing.
"Come, all you creatures, and drink.
Come to the edge of the darkness and drink,
drink of me all through the depths of the night.

I long for these living waters."

Where did I find the hidden source at last?
I found her brimming within the bread of life,
        hidden in the depths of the night.

— St. John of the Cross

You do very well . . . to seek him always as one hidden.

You honor God greatly, and indeed come near to him, when you hold him to be nobler and deeper than anything you can attain.

So do not settle down and try to find a corner in what your mind and heart can grasp . . .

And do not be like many heartless people who have a low opinion of God: they think that when they cannot understand him or sense him or feel him, he is further away—when the truth is more the opposite; it is when you understand him less clearly that you are coming closer to him.

— St. John of the Cross,
in "The Spiritual Canticle"

And to bring peace to passion and lay it
    to rest . . .
endeavor always to be inclined
not to what is easier, but to what
    is harder . . .
not to what is more, but to what
    is less . . .
not to wanting something, but to
    wanting nothing . . .
longing to enter in utter nakedness,
and emptiness,
and poverty,
for Christ.

— St. John of the Cross,
in *Ascent to Mount Carmel*

On a dark night,
inflamed by love-longing—
O exquisite risk!—
Undetected I slipped away,
my house, at last, grown still.

Secure in the darkness,
I climbed the secret ladder in disguise—
O exquisite risk!—
concealed by the darkness,
my house, at last, grown still.

That sweet night: a secret.
Nobody saw me;
I did not see a thing.
No other light, no other guide,
than the one burning in my heart.

This light led the way
more clearly than the risen sun
to where he was waiting for me
—the one I knew so intimately—
in a place where no one could find us.

Saint John of the Cross

O night, that guided me!
O night, sweeter than sunrise!
O night, that joined lover with Beloved,
Lover transformed in Beloved!

Upon my blossoming breast,
which I cultivated just for him,
he drifted into sleep,
and while I caressed him,
a cedar breeze touched the air.

Wind blew down from the tower,
parting the locks of his hair.
With his gentle hand
he wounded my neck
and all my senses were suspended.

I lost myself. Forgot myself.
I lay my face against the Beloved's face.
Everything fell away and I left
    myself behind,
abandoning my cares
among the lilies, forgotten.

— St. John of the Cross

✐ Extreme Beliefs ✐

The more purely spiritual the experiences that touch the soul, the more extreme are her beliefs about them.

Pure spiritual experiences, says John, have this quality:

When the soul gets into spiritual trouble, she thinks she will never get out of it. She feels hopeless and lost. Everywhere she looks, forward and backward along the timeline of her life, she sees nothing but misery. She knows without a doubt that it will always be this way—dark.

Then, when spiritual blessings come streaming down on her once more, showering the soul with grace, it seems to her that all her troubles are over forever, and she will not fall for the illusion of sorrow again. Wherever she looks she sees only light.

⁓ᴍᴏ **This Earth a Bow** ⁓ᴍᴏ

You let
my sufferings cease,
for there was no one who could cure them.

Now let my eyes behold your face for you are our only love.

My spirit's body is rising near—this earth a bow
that shot me;

now lift me into your arms as something precious
that you dropped.

My only suffering, from this day forth,will be your divine
beauty,

and you will constantly cure my blessed sight each time
you bring your face so near to mine
and call me
bride . . .

—In the spirit of St. John of the Cross,
Daniel Ladinsky

However much saintly teachers have
discovered and holy people understood . . .
the greater part remains to be said, and even
to be understood.

There is much to fathom in Christ.

He is like a huge mine with seam after
seam of treasures. However deep you dig,
never will you find an end or come to
a conclusion.

— St. John of the Cross,
in "The Spiritual Canticle"

Chapter Four

Love

Y ou are a moth, engaged to be married to fire. You dress in your finest garments and head for the altar where your Beloved is waiting.

"Come," says the flame, extending his blazing hand.

Inexorably drawn, you rush into his embrace. You have waited all your life for this burning.

Divine union is a ridiculous thing.

You ache with an ineffable yearning no human being can meet, no sensual pleasure can fill, no earthly success can touch. You languish in your unrelenting longing for connection with the Beloved. You go to extraordinary lengths and take outrageous risks for a single glimpse of the hem of his robe.

You think he is in love with you. This hope urges you on.

You think he has forgotten you. The despair crushes you.

And then, at last: your wedding day. The time has come for you to meet your Beloved and become one with him.

But no one told you this union would require your total annihilation.

When lover and Beloved merge at last, lover is completely absorbed in Beloved. No separate self remains to enjoy the fruits of that melding.

May we all be burned to death!

❧

Flame, alive, compelling,
yet tender past all telling,
reaching the secret center of my soul!
Since now evasion's over,
finish your work, my Lover,
break the last thread, wound me and
    make me whole!

Burn that is for my healing!
Wound of delight past feeling!
Ah, gentle hand whose touch is a caress,
foretaste of heaven conveying
and every debt repaying:
slaying, you give me life for
death's distress.

O lamps of fire bright-burning
with splendid brilliance, turning
deep caverns of my soul to pools of light!
Once shadowed, dim, unknowing,
now their strange new-found glowing
gives warmth and radiance for my
Love's delight.

Ah! gentle and so loving
you wake within me, proving
that you are there in secret and alone;
your fragrant breathing stills me,
your grace, your glory fills me,
so tenderly your love becomes my own.

— St. John of the Cross,
in *Living Flame of Love*

hat is this dark magic that transforms something ordinary into sheer radiance?

Divine light, John says, is like fire.

When a flame touches a piece of fuel, it warms it and drives out the moisture. The wood begins to shed the tears it has held inside itself.

Soon the wood begins to blacken and crumble. It grows dark and unlovely. Maybe a foul odor drifts from it, a black smoke that chokes anyone nearby.

Little by little, the flames draw all impurities from the heart of the wood, emptying it of all the "unsavory accidents" that characterize the elemental state of the wood and defy its true destiny.

Finally, moving steadily inward from the outside, the fire penetrates the core of the wood, heating it up and enkindling it so thoroughly that the wood becomes fire. The fire transforms the wood into itself.

Saint John of the Cross

Fire makes wood as beautiful as fire is.
The divine light makes our souls burst
into flame and turns us into divine light.

❧

The capacity of these caverns
    [the human spirit] is deep,
because that which can fill them is
    deep, infinite;
and that is God.

So in a sense
their capacity will be infinite;
so their thirst is infinite,
and their hunger is deep and infinite,
and their sense of pain
and disintegration
is infinite death
when the soul is alert
to receive what will fill it.

— St. John of the Cross,
in *Living Flame of Love*

❧

Love

The power and intensity of love have
this quality. Love makes everything
seem possible.

Love believes everyone must feel this
same passion.

Love cannot understand how anyone
could waste their time with anything other
than seeking the Beloved . . .

Like a lioness or a she-bear that goes
looking for her lost cubs, the wounded soul
goes anxiously forth in search of her God . . .

— St. John of the Cross
in *Dark Night of the Soul*

The power and tenacity of Love is great, for love captures and binds God himself! Happy is the loving soul, since she possesses God for her prisoner, and he is surrendered to all her desires.

God is such that those who act with love and friendship toward him will make him do all they desire, but if they act otherwise there is no speaking to him or power with him, even though they go to extremes.

Yet by love they bind him with one hair.

— St. John of the Cross,
in "The Spiritual Canticle"

How incredible and sad it is that the soul, in her weakness and impurity, mistakes the soft and gentle hand of God as being heavy and hostile!

He does not press down or load up the soul but only touches her and touches her mercifully, not to castigate the soul but to grant her favors.

— St. John of the Cross,
in *Dark Night of the Soul*

You looked with love upon me
And deep within your eyes
   imprinted grace;
This mercy set me free,
Held in your love's embrace,
To lift my eyes adoring to your grace.

— St. John of the Cross,
in "The Spiritual Canticle"

ᕯᔿᕧᕯ Naked Wisdom ᕯᔿᕧᕯ

So, you encountered the wisdom of divine love?

I did.

What did it look like?

Look like? The wisdom of love came naked. It was not dressed in the clothes of any physical image. It bore no content. None. It bypassed my intellect, transcended my senses, overrode my will, and penetrated me directly. How could I possibly report on the color of its garments? It shed every scrap on my threshold and threw itself into my arms and entered me.

How can you be so sure the wisdom of divine love was inside you? It sounds so vague, like a cloud, like a dream, like an error.

I have never been more certain of anything in my life. There is nothing vague about it. Just because it was naked does not make it anything less than perfectly beautiful and perfectly clear. Its flavor

lingers on my tongue, changing the way I
taste everything. The language of love has
no words.

Try. Please try.

Listen. It would be as if you saw
something no one had ever seen before.
In fact, no one had even seen anything
remotely similar. It was the most marvelous
thing you had ever encountered, a thing
that changed you forever. And yet, even in
the midst of fully experiencing it, utterly
enjoying it, and completely understanding
it, how could you ever begin to describe it?
Mere metaphor does not come close. All you
could do would be to stammer, like Moses:
"Ah, ah, ah . . ."

No words?

The wisdom of divine love silences the soul.

Mountains have heights and they are
affluent, vast, graceful, bright and fragrant.

These mountains are what my Beloved
is to me.

Lonely valleys are quiet, pleasant, cool,
shady, and flowing with fresh waters; in the
variety of their groves and in the sweet song
of the birds, they afford abundant recreation
and delight to the senses, and in their solitude
and silence they refresh and give rest.

These valleys are what my Beloved is
to me.

— St. John of the Cross,
in "The Spiritual Canticle"

Love
107

O thickets, densely-trammelled,
Which my love's hand has sown along
    the height:
O field of green, enamelled
With blossoms, tell me right
If he has passed across you in his flight.

Diffusing showers of grace
In haste among these groves his path he took,
And only with his face,
Glancing around the place,
Has clothed them in his beauty with a look.

— St. John of the Cross
in "The Spiritual Canticle"

Speak, earth and sky; speak, seas;
speak, mountains and valleys and hills;
speak, vineyards, fields of grain, and
    olive groves;
speak, herbs and flowers; speak, meadows;
tell me where He is
who has given you beauty and being.

Angels that gazing rejoice,
spirits that love and possess,
brides that this Bridegroom desires,
and whose sweet embraces you seek,
tell me where he is,
who has given you beauty and being . . .

Birds that resound with sweet song,
serpents, animals and sea creatures,
tell me if you know where He is
who has given you beauty and being.

— St. John of the Cross

Love

My beloved, the mountains,
lonely wooded valleys,
rare islands,
thundering rivers,
the whisper of love, carried by the breeze.

The tranquil night
at one with the rising dawn,
the silence of music,
the mighty sound of solitude
the feast where love makes all new.

— St. John of the Cross,
in "The Spiritual Canticle"

On the highest steps of love, the secret
ladder is not so secret anymore.

Love generates amazing effects.
Everything is revealed to the soul! On this
final step of clear vision, where the soul
finds God resting at the top of the ladder, she
merges completely with him and nothing
remains hidden from her.

Christ said, "On that day, you shall ask
me nothing." Until that day, no matter how
high the soul climbs, something will remain
secret, in proportion to her separation from
the divine essence . . .

Love is like a fire. It rises perpetually
upward, yearning to be absorbed at its
very center . . .

And so the soul will be called, and so
shall she be, God by participation.

— St. John of the Cross,
in *Dark Night of the Soul*

To Those Songs

Your body is a divine stream,
as is your spirit.

When your two great rivers merge, one voice is found
and the earth applauds
in excitement.

Shrines are erected to those songs
the hand and heart have sung
as they served
the world

with a love, a love
we cherish.

—In the spirit of St. John of the Cross,
Daniel Ladinsky

I do not doubt that some people,
not understanding this,
nor knowing the reality of it,
will either disbelieve it,
or think it exaggerated,
or reckon it less than it in fact is.

But to all of these I answer,
that the Father of Lights,
whose hand is not shortened,
and who pours himself out abundantly,
without partiality.
wherever he finds space,
like a ray of sunlight,
and joyfully discloses himself
to the people on the footpaths
    and highways—
this God does not hesitate
or disdain to find his delight
among the children of men.

— St. John of the Cross,
in *Living Flame of Love*

This he did when he became a man, lifting man up in the beauty of God, and so lifting up all creatures in him . . .

In this raising up in the Son's incarnation and in the glory of his resurrection according to the flesh, the Father gave creatures not just a partial beauty; we can say that he entirely clothed them in beauty and dignity.

— St. John of the Cross,
in "The Spiritual Canticle"

Why Does Not
the Church Tell You?

. . . Why does not my sacred church tell you:

God only sees

Himself.

—In the spirit of St. John of the Cross,
Daniel Ladinsky

Frequent combing gives the hair more luster and makes it easier to comb.

A soul who frequently examines her thoughts, words, and deeds, which are her hair, doing all things for the love of God, will have lustrous hair.

Then the Spouse will look upon the neck of the bride and thereby be captivated, and will be wounded by one of her eyes, that is, by the purity of intention she has in all she does.

If in combing hair one wants it to have luster, one begins from the crown.

All our works must begin from the crown (the love of God) if we wish them to be pure and lustrous.

— St. John of the Cross,
The Maxims of Love

*Rare, useful
learning programs
with you in mind*

THE
SOUNDS TRUE
CATALOG

... is your direct source for
inspirational and informative
audio and video recordings
about meditation, psychology,
spirituality and religion, health
and healing, relationships,
personal discovery, creativity,
sacred music, and much more.
Call toll free 800-333-9185, visit
www.soundstrue.com, or mail
this card to Sounds True.

Yes, please send me a free catalog:

PRINT NAME

ADDRESS

CITY   STATE   ZIP

EMAIL ADDRESS (Learn about new releases and special offers.
Note: We never share email addresses with other companies.)

May we send a free catalog to one of your friends?

PRINT FRIEND'S NAME

ADDRESS

CITY   STATE   ZIP

STB04

BUSINESS REPLY MAIL

FIRST-CLASS MAIL   PERMIT NO. 493   BOULDER, CO.

POSTAGE WILL BE PAID BY ADDRESSEE:

SOUNDS TRUE
CATALOG

PO BOX 8010
BOULDER CO 80306-9886

Love greatly those who speak against you and do not love you, because in this way love will come to birth in a heart that has none.

That is what God does with us: he loves us, that we might love him, through the love he has for us.

— St. John of the Cross

Pregnant with the Word
the handmaid of the Holy One
comes walking down the road.
Will you offer her
shelter for the night?

— St John of the Cross

Beloved

God held
the earth as if it were His lover
and spoke with the most tender of feelings
to all in existence as He spoke
to me,

"Look, dear son, I have made a bride for you,
but she is shy; so how are you
to consummate?

I want all souls to consummate with me,
so I devised a plan:

As each soul nears heaven differences will dissolve to such
a sublime extent that when the heart looks upon
any object in this world it
will cry 'Beloved'

and passionately run into
an embrace with
me."

Saint John of the Cross

That blessed grace I now know.
I now see my Beloved
everywhere.

—In the spirit of St. John of the Cross,
Daniel Ladinsky

Closing Prayer

O, Saint John of the Cross,
I can no longer hear
the familiar song of God's flute,
a sound that lured me long ago
from the safety of my mother's house,
out into the Garden in the middle of
   the night
where the Holy One told me he would
   be waiting.

O, friend of the hidden Beloved,
my thoughts cannot find their way
back to him anymore.
His name has become nothing but
   a word.
I have cultivated my faith
with enthusiasm and care,
yet it lies withered at my feet.

O, wise brother in God,
remind me
that this void is plenitude,

this aridity abundance,
this darkness pure light.
I cannot see my hands in front of my face.
I can no longer pray or meditate.
I can't think or believe.
All I can do is breathe.

O, John of the Cross,
breathe with me.
Sit with me in this deep silence.
Give me the strength
not to turn away from the pain,
the pain of unknowing.
Help me to unknow
everything I thought I knew
about the Holy One.

O, you lover of the night,
teach me to embrace the darkness.
Let me lie with you under the black sky
and memorize the way
the stars arrange themselves
to the glory of their Creator.
Help me to burn my map,

throw off my sandals,
and make my way home blind.
My eyes have only misled me.

O, joyful captive of the Holy One,
show me how to surrender.
abandon myself to the loving embrace
of an invisible Beloved,
to transform the prison cell of my old self
into the wedding chamber of the Lord,
and, in dying to who I thought I was,
being born into the one
God has been longing for.

O, master of silence,
give me the courage
to pour the contents of my cup
on the ground at God's feet:
all attachments to spiritual feelings,
all ideas about the spiritual path.
Let me sit quietly in my shattering,
exploring the total circumference
of my nothingness.

O, wild man of God,
share with me the secret
of the blazing fire
hidden just beneath the surface
of your calm heart.
Recite to me
your passionate love poetry,
the language of my own yearning.
Remind me
that only by letting go of all hope
can I ever come to receive
the fullness of God's love:
a tender filling
of every fiber
of my broken-open soul.

Amen.

— Mirabai Starr

Sources

❧

Bibliography

Campbell, Roy (trans.). *St. John of the Cross: Poems.* New York: Random House, 1960.

Canatsey, Kenneth, trans. *A Bilingual Edition of Poems by St. John of the Cross: Spiritual Songs and Ballads.* Lewiston, NY: The Edwin Mellen Press, 2003.

Farrington, Tim. "A Hell of Mercy," *The Sun Magazine,* March 2001.

Gaucher, Guy. *John and Therese: Flames of Love.* Staten Island, NY: Alba House, 1999.

Kavanaugh, Kieran and Otilio Rodriguez, trans. *The Collected Works of St. John of the Cross.* Washington, D.C.: ICS Publications, 1991.

Ladinsky, Daniel. *Love Poems from God.* New York: Penguin Group, 2002.

Matthew, Iain. *The Impact of God: Soundings from St. John of the Cross.* Oxford: Hodder & Stoughton, 1995.

Nims, John Frederick, trans. *The Poems of St. John of the Cross.* Chicago: University of Chicago Press, 1989.

Starr, Mirabai, trans. *Dark Night of the Soul.* New York: Riverhead Books, 2002.

Credits

⚜ Art Credits ⚜

⚘

About Sounds True

Sounds True was founded in 1985 with a clear vision: to disseminate spiritual wisdom. Located in Boulder, Colorado, Sounds True publishes teaching programs that are designed to educate, uplift, and inspire. We work with many of the leading spiritual teachers, thinkers, healers, and visionary artists of our time.

To receive a free catalog of tools and teachings for personal and spiritual transformation, please visit www.soundstrue.com, call toll-free 800-333-9185, or write to us at the address below.

SOUNDS TRUE
PO BOX 8010 / BOULDER, CO 80306